Dylan at Newport, 1965

Music, Myth, and Un-Meaning

Dylan at Newport, 1965

Music, Myth, and Un-Meaning

By
Edward Renehan

2015
New Street Communications, LLC
Wickford, Rhode Island
newstreetcommunications.com

Contents

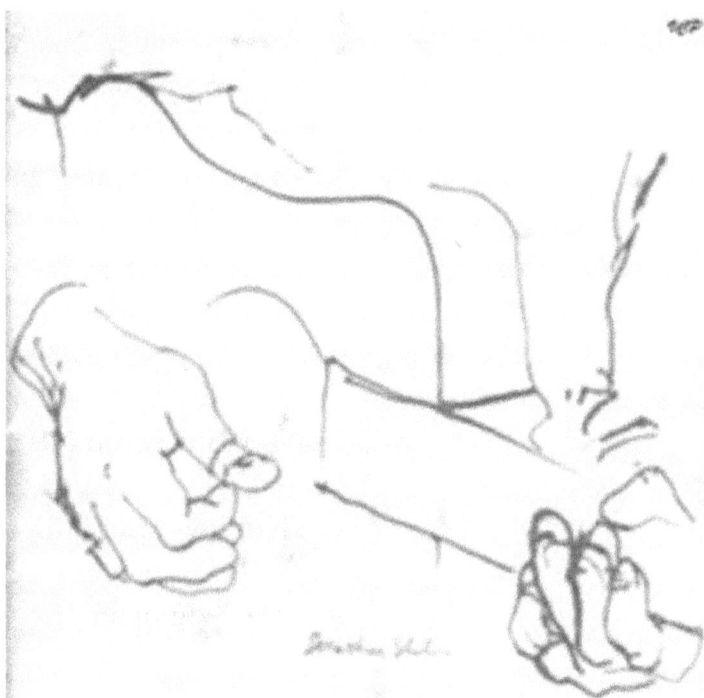

newport folk festival
july 22-25   1965

Pivot Point

*For me, the lame part of the Sixties was the political
part, the social part. The real part was the spiritual part.*

- Jerry Garcia

"Mention of `the Sixties' rouses strong emotions
even in those who were already old when the Sixties
began and those who were not even born when the
Sixties ended." So wrote the eminent cultural histor-
ian Arthur Marwick. "For some it is a golden age, for
others a time when the old secure framework of
morality, authority, and discipline disintegrated. In
the eyes of the far left, it is the era when revolution
was at hand, only to be betrayed by the feebleness of
the faithful and the trickery of the enemy; to the
radical right, an era of subversion and moral tur-
pitude. What happened between the late Fifties and
the early Seventies has been subject to political

polemic, nostalgic mythologizing, and downright misrepresentations."

Emphasis on mythologizing and, I might add, gross over-simplification.

In the popular mind – our *tribal memory*, if you will – a number of key moments and utterances have come to define the arc of the Sixties.

Politically, these include the August 1963 Civil Rights March on Washington and Dr. King's "I Have a Dream" Speech, the November 1963 assassination of JFK, the 1965 assassination of Malcom X, the 1968 assassinations of Dr. King and RFK, the riots at the 1968 Democratic Convention, the subsequent trial of the Chicago Seven, and the shootings at Kent State (a fundamental part of the Sixties even though they happened in May of 1970). Culturally, these include such "watershed" events as the so-called "Summer of Love" and the Woodstock Festival.

Individuals too have become iconic benchmarks. Fundamental aspects of the Sixties come to mind when we recall Timothy Leary and his cult of awakening one's mind through LSD, Ken Kesey (both as a novelist and as an LSD evangelist via the famous "Acid Tests"), Jack Kerouac (primarily a Fifties writer who, despite himself, became a Sixties phenomenon and hero to a generation he did not pretend to understand), Wavy Gravy, Allen Ginsberg, Jerry Garcia, Abbie Hoffman, Janice Joplin, Jerry Rubin, and so on.

Generalities are easy, especially when it comes to what has gone before. While we are more likely to see present events as nuanced and conditional, we tend to view events of the past as absolute. So far as our tribal memory and imagination are concerned, we like our history rendered in straight and definitely drawn lines. Black and white, with few if any grays. We like fast, blunt, and all-too-simple facts. You know, stuff like: The Civil War was all about freeing the slaves; and the stock market crash of "Black Friday" *caused* the Great Depression.

One key way we simplify the past is to take notable or notorious (but nearly always dramatic) events and turn them into imaginary dividers in the timeline of tribal memory. We bracket eras and mini-eras with these events, thus endowing them with a grossly overstated degree of historical and cultural significance. But truth be told, the 1963 March on Washington, for example, neither began nor ended anything. The event represented just one more step in a complex, ongoing struggle that had begun years earlier and, in many ways, continues to this day. The same can be said of countless other moments and events which at first glance seem seminal.

One of the most famous such moments of the Sixties, one which continues to this day to be grossly misconstrued, mistold, and loaded with undeserved meaning, is the night in July of 1965 when Bob Dylan played an electric set – or at least *tried* to play an electric set – at the Newport Folk Festival: an event after which, supposedly, the culture of the Sixties was never quite the same again.

Even Dylan's most pre-eminent chronicler Sean Wilentz has mischaracterized this evening as the night when "[Alan] Lomax along with Pete Seeger led the old guard that objected to the blasts of white-boy electricity, including Dylan's." Seeger biographer David Dunaway speaks of Dylan understanding that at Newport "the electric guitar meant a declaration of war" and that, intensely ambitious, he sought publicity by smuggling "rock into the citadel of folk music." In this narrative, battle lines were drawn, a fight waged, and a revolution begun.

The over-simplification is too attractive to resist. Our tribal memory *absolutely yearns* for Dylan's abbreviated, 15-minute performance to be a pivot point not just from acoustic to electric, but also from traditional to commercial, from topical to cynical, and from roots to revolution. We also want Newport to be a "citadel of folk music,"and to be comfortable with any number of other safe, easy assumptions.

For this symbology to work, however, we need an "old guard" to rebel against, and a youthful "new guard" to do the rising up. We also need to believe that traditional acoustic music cannot be (and was not at that time already) commercial, that electric music can never be traditional, that electric music is always commercial, that the Newport Fest (only a few years old) represented some sort of "hallowed ground" of acoustic music, and that various other straight lines apply.

They don't.

Dylan at Newport, 1965

6

The Purist and the Pirate

The world is filled with people who are no longer needed – and who try to make slaves of all of us – they have their music and we have ours.
- Woody Guthrie

Attendees at an afternoon Newport Folk Festival performance on Friday, July 23rd, 1965 were treated to a spectacle not on the official schedule of entertainments. Not far from the small stage upon which the *Blues Origins and Offshoots* workshop was in progress, Bob Dylan's manager Al Grossman and pre-eminent folklorist Alan Lomax exchanged punches and ended up wrestling, pounding each other in an out-and-out brawl – one which had to be broken up by brawny drummer Sam Lay and other members of the Paul Butterfield Blues Band, who restrained each furious man in turn before they killed one another.

The older of the two, Alan Lomax (1915-2002) had been surrounded from the cradle by the rawest, purest, truest, and most utterly-authentic American folk music. His father, Texan folklorist John Lomax (1867-1948), was the first great pioneer collector of folk songs in the United States. As a mere boy Alan accompanied his father into farm fields and prisons where together, using primitive equipment, they recorded worksongs, spirituals, and blues for a growing collection which wound up forming the principal part of the Library of Congress's Archive of American Folk Song.

Alan was just 18 in 1933 when he and his father graduated from a very elementary wax cylinder recording device to a bulky, 315-pound uncoated aluminum disk recorder which they loaded into a black sedan for expeditions across the American South. Alan's father in particular liked to visit Southern prisons (all of them disproportionatly black, of course) where, as the elder Lomax put it in a grant application, prisoners "thrown on their own resources ... still sing, especially the long-term prisoners who have been confined for years and who have not yet been influenced by jazz and the radio ..." As Alan was to recall:

The whole of the great secular songs of the

blacks were considered sinful. You could be kicked out of the church for singing them. It was difficult for us to get at this rich and unknown treasure trove of American music and lyricism because people were scared to sing them. So we decided to go where the devils were — the people who were beyond redemption — and we found them in the prisons and we recorded a whole literature, an enormous song bag of new kinds of tunes and melodies and all sorts of things.

The focus, in other words, was to collect genuinely organic, unadulterated songs emerging out of the true folk process, uncorrupted by pop culture. Thus prisons, and the prisoners long-confined within them, served the collectors' purposes well. It was in Louisiana's Angola Prison that, in 1933, father and son encountered the black 12-string guitar player Huddie Ledbetter (*Lead Belly* or *Leadbelly*). Ledbetter had experienced his first prison chain gang in 1915 on a charge of carrying a weapon, and then did seven years for the 1918 murder of a relative. When Lomax father and son found him, he was incarcerated on another conviction for attempted murder. He received a pardon in 1934, partially through the advocacy of John Lomax.

Father and son were both purists when it came to indigenous music and indigenous cultures. They held that the ultimate sin was the commercialization of culture. In general, they believed true tradition and native art to be in grave danger of perishing under the increasing influence of mass-produced, homogenized entertainment. True art, they believed, flourished best at the local rather than the national or international levels. Genuine culture – as opposed to plastic culture – derived from regional landscapes, vocations, turmoils, and spiritual beliefs. Mass communications and centralized commercial entertainment were suspect – tools too convenient for the stomping out of local traditions. The products of Tin Pan Alley paled in comparison to authentic folk music with all of its spontaneous, uncontrived, spiritual (in fact, nearly Jungian) depths.

After his father's death in 1948, Alan Lomax looked on disdainfully as what some (never Alan) called folk music emerged as a commercial product itself – in his eyes a crime sometimes perpetuated by his own close friends.

Lomax was grim and disapproving when, in 1950, Pete Seeger's popular *Weavers* quartet (Seeger, Ronnie Gilbert, Lee Hays, and Fred Hellerman) scored a number one hit for Decca with a saccharine, watered-down, waltz-like version of Ledbetter's "Goodnight, Irene." The recording charted on *Billboard* in June of 1950, and stayed on the chart for 25 weeks.

Not only did the Weavers, under the direction of producer Gordon Jenkins, replace traditional folk instruments with a full orchestra, they also revised Ledbetter's original lyrics to make them more accept-able to a wide and easily offended audience. For example, they removed a verse containing the phrase "take morphine and die," and in the chorus they replaced the more suggestive "I'll *get* you in my dreams" with "I'll see you in my dreams." Sinatra covered the Weavers version of the song one month after release of the Weavers recording. To this day, the corrupted Weavers version of "Goodnight, Irene" remains the one sung most often, with Ledbetter's starker and far more brilliant original version generally forgotten.

Lomax was similarly disapproving when the Weavers achieved other hits with popularized, sanitized versions of such folk songs as "On Top of Old Smokey," "Rock Island Line," and Woody Guthrie's "So Long, It's Been Good to Know Ya."

Lomax had played a key role in "discovering" Guthrie, whom he considered to be an "authentic" balladeer: a bard whose art had been developed and distilled among working people and whose creations contained no commercial pretentions whatsoever.

Guthrie was, unlike Seeger, not a Harvard-educated "city-singer" who sang working-class songs with which he had no experiential connection. Rather, Guthrie was a genuine Okie right out of *The Grapes of Wrath* – a man who, when he wrote and sang of dust storms and life as a migrant worker and travels as a vagabond hopping freights, spoke from actual experience. Real life. *His* life.

Per prominent Guthrie biographer Ed Cray, when Lomax first encountered Guthrie in the year 1940, he was "overwhelmed. Guthrie was not only singing folk songs, he was writing his own, songs that reflected Lomax's own belief in a 'New America,' a nation in which the working people expressed themselves through folk culture." Alan Lomax considered Guthrie an untutored "natural genius ... the kind of person who wrote the great ballads about Jesse James and Sam Bass," and who, in more ancient times, had originated such anonymous masterpieces as "Barbara Allen," sending them on their way to be further honed and refined by countless more anonymous singers through the centuries.

Unlike those early artists, Guthrie was not anonymous. But his sound was as raw as any Lomax might have captured with his portable recorder in any tavern or migrant camp, and his art just as organic. Lomax thought it a pity when Guthrie's songs, like Ledbetter's, wound up commercialized: effectively destroyed for the profit of the same media machine which, so far as Lomax was concerned, threatened the essence of the true folk culture out of which both artists had emerged.

Of course, many more popularizers followed the Weavers, these including the Rooftop Singers, the New Christy Minstrels, Harry Belafonte, the Brothers Four, and the Chad Mitchell Trio. In 1961, Seeger began to emerge from a period of blacklisting by signing a lucrative contract with Columbia Records.

Soon thereafter he began introducing Columbia producer John Hammond to other folk artists which the label signed. Perhaps the most prominent of these were the Clancy Brothers and Tommy Makem, with their bold (and heretofore unpolished) renditions of classic songs out of the Irish tradition – songs they'd learned from grandparents, parents, and neighbors on waterfronts and in kitchens when still children.

Other major labels joined the profitable party. In due course, the Kingston Trio and Peter, Paul, and Mary had hits, respectively, with such Seeger-penned songs as "Where Have All the Flowers Gone?" (released 1961) and "If I Had a Hammer" (released 1962).

And now the "folk-boom" was truly on its way. Hammond signed the young Bob Dylan to Columbia in late 1961. Dylan's first self-titled album came out in March of '62. Peter, Paul, and Mary scored a hit in the summer of 1963 with Dylan's "Blowin' In the Wind," that single selling more than 300,000 copies. Around this same time, ABC launched a weekly television program, *Hootenanny*: essentially an acoustic version of *American Bandstand*.

Amid all this, Albert Grossman (1926-1986), eight years younger than Lomax, emerged as a dominant and dominating impresario. The son of a Chicago tailor, trained as an economist at Roosevelt University, Grossman had founded the folk-club *The Gate of Horn* in Chicago during the 1950s, where such artists as Jim (later *Roger*) McGuinn got their start. From there he moved into management.

Always an astute businessman, Grossman quickly developed a model which allowed him to profit from all aspects of his client's careers. He managed their affairs across the board, including bookings, at a 25% (as opposed to the standard 15%) commission. He took a piece of their publishing rights. He negotiated their record deals. And he owned the studios in which they recorded. Sometimes he even assembled the acts himself. Peter, Paul, and Mary, for example, were a trio invented by Grossman. They'd never sung together until Grossman herded them into a room and told them to do so.

Grossman signed Dylan in 1962, and it was under his aegis that Peter, Paul, and Mary made their blockbuster recording of Dylan's "Blowin' In the

Wind." Eventually Grossman's clients came to include The Band, Janis Joplin, and many others.

Howard Sounes sums up Grossman well in his excellent *Down the Highway: The Life of Bob Dylan*:

> Grossman's sharp business sense ran contrary to the idealism of the folk revival, with its undercurrent of left-wing politics and its fixation with authenticity. To be a dustbowl poet, like Woody Guthrie … was glorious, while making a fortune from the music of the working people was anathema. Many performers disliked Grossman. Dave Van Ronk says Grossman derived pleasure from corrupting young artists and points out that one of his favorite books was *The Magic Christian* by Terry Southern, a darkly comic novel the gist of which was everyone had a price.

Lomax and Grossman were diametrically opposed in their interests, ambitions, and concerns. But they had similar temperaments. Each was aggressive, acerbic, and enormously self-confident. Neither had an ego problem. Each was completely confident in his own cultural, aesthetic, and philosophical judgments. For one, music was a sacred artifact. For the other, it was big business.

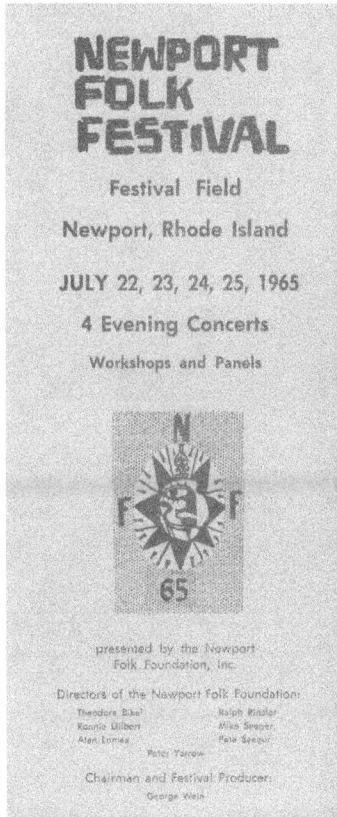

NEWPORT FOLK FESTIVAL

Festival Field

Newport, Rhode Island

JULY 22, 23, 24, 25, 1965

4 Evening Concerts

Workshops and Panels

presented by the Newport
Folk Foundation, Inc.

Directors of the Newport Folk Foundation:

Theodore Bikel   Ralph Rinzler
Ronnie Gilbert   Mike Seeger
Alan Lomax   Pete Seeger
          Peter Yarrow

Chairman and Festival Producer:
George Wein

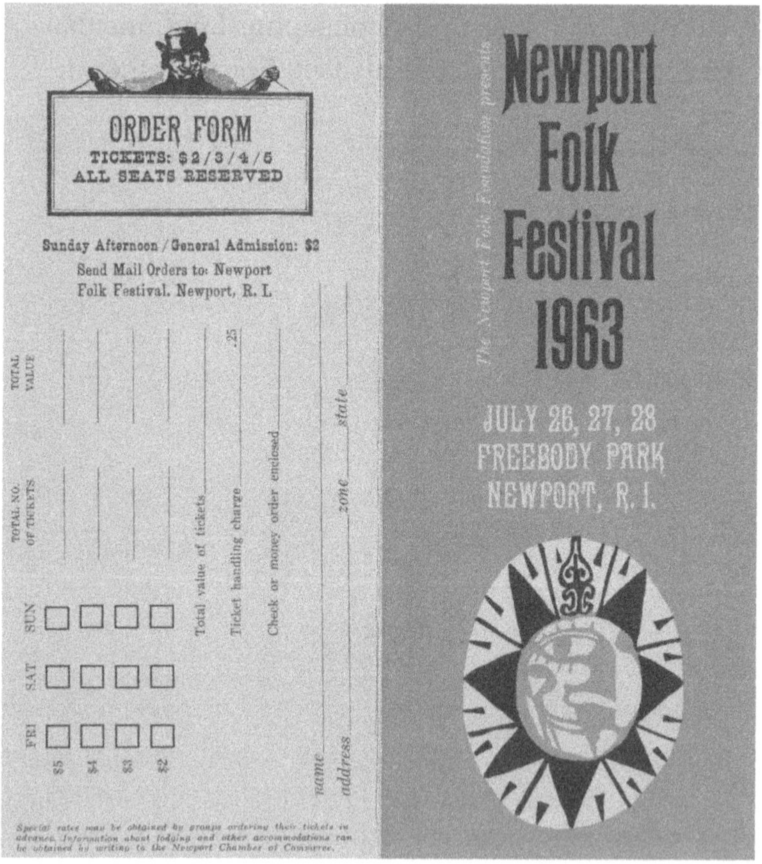

General admission $2.00 – 1963.

The Evolution of a Festival, And an Artist

This is America, you live in it, you let it happen.
- Thomas Pynchon, *The Crying of Lot 49*

Jazz impresario George Wein founded the Newport Folk Festival in 1959. Joining him in this venture was a board comprised of Pete Seeger, Theodore Bikel, Albert Grossman, and Oscar Brand. The Folk event was contrived as a sister to the Newport Jazz Festival, which Wein had launched in 1954 in collaboration with tobacco heirs and Newport residents Louis and Elaine Lorillard.

From its first year, the Festival – largely through the influence of Toshi and Pete Seeger, but with the approval of the entire board – worked on a model which eschewed the star system. Programs featured genuine, non-professional performers of traditional music (the type of which Lomax approved) along with celebrity city-singers (such as the types which

Grossman managed), all of whom were paid just a small minimum performance fee plus travel expenses. In addition to main stage events, the Festival featured numerous workshops focusing on various traditions, instruments, and skills.

As the *New York Times's* Tom Piazza notes: "In the early 1960's, the Newport Folk Festival was the central event of any given year for those who loved folk music. From around the country, college guitar pickers, old-time fiddlers and banjo players, Appalachian clog dancers, blues singers from deepest Mississippi, folk stars like Pete Seeger and Joan Baez, gospel singers, Cajun bands and bluegrass groups all converged on that Rhode Island enclave of wealth and privilege for concerts, workshops and jam sessions."

Although today held at Fort Adams State Park on the Newport waterfront, the Festival was in its early years held mostly at Freebody Park, with a few events taking place at a couple of other venues, including the Newport Casino (now the Tennis Hall of Fame). In 1965 however, in anticipation of the Festival's largest crowd ever, the venue was changed to the so-called

"Festival Field" in the north end of the city, off Connell Highway.

The first Festival of 1959 included such performers as Seeger, Odetta, Jean Ritchie, John Jacob Niles, Sonny Terry & Brownie McGhee, Earl Scruggs, Bob Gibson, and the New Lost City Ramblers, with Seeger and Scruggs being the most commercially viable of all these headliners. During one evening concert, Bob Gibson brought on the young, unknown, and un-billed Joan Baez to sing two songs, thus launching her career. Additional artists included Martha Schlamme, Leon Bibb, Tommy Makem and Pat Clancy, Barbara Dane, Oscar Brand, Frank Hamilton, folksong collector Frank Warner, Cynthia Gooding, and Ed McCurdy. 1960 saw a similar range of musicians, including Cisco Houston. For various reasons, there were no Festivals in '61 or '62.

Dylan first showed up in 1963, participating in two workshops (one on *Ballads* and one on *Topical Songs and New Songwriters*), as well as the Friday evening main stage concert, where he appeared on a bill with Sonny Terry & Brownie McGhee, the Freedom Singers, Bill Monroe & The Bluegrass Boys, Jean Redpath, Doc Watson, Peter, Paul, and Mary,

and others. Additional Festival performers throughout the weekend included Seeger (with whom Dylan
dueted on "Ye Playboys and Playgirls" during the
Topical Song and New Songwriters workshop), Mississippi John Hurt, John Hammond Jr., John Lee
Hooker, Dave Van Ronk, Maybelle Carter, Ramblin'
Jack Elliott, Ian & Sylvia, the Rooftop Singers, the
Staples Singers, and Judy Collins. Interspersed among
these were a host of nonprofessional performers of
traditional music, mostly appearing in sideline workshops.

A similar pattern was to apply going forward
through '64, '65, and onward, but with an increasing
preponderance of attention being given to "main
stage" performers rather than the more obscure and
"authentic" pickers and singers.

During early Festival years, most modern singer-
songwriters had – under the looming influence of
Seeger and the now hospitalized Woody Guthrie –
fixated on topical material. The link between the
modern folk movement (no matter how much
commercialized) and the Civil Rights and anti-war
movements of the 1960s was not to be denied.
Newport workshops focused not only on Cajun

fiddling and alternate banjo tunings, but also such topics as *Songs for Group Singing During Protest Actions*.

Left-wing politics had formed the throbbing heart of the urban folk movement ever since the 1940s, and its imprint remained. Thus, at Newport and elsewhere, protest stood as the prevailing theme of contemporary songs performed by the likes of Tom Paxton, Phil Ochs, Dylan and others who were seen as crafting works of lyrical and musical art in the tradition of Joe Hill and other radical songmakers.

But Dylan's Festival performances in '64 began to challenge this paradigm. In a way, his '64 performances were even more controversial than would be his "going electric" one year later.

At the '64 Festival, Dylan highlighted his latest crop of songs, these from his fourth Columbia album *Another Side of Bob Dylan*, scheduled for release just a week or two after the Festival. All of these were far more personal and poetic than political. The songs included "My Back Pages," "Ballad in Plain D," "Chimes of Freedom," and "All I Really Want To Do." Dylan also performed "Mr. Tambourine Man," which would not be released on an album until 1965's

Bringing It All Back Home. The closest some of the songs came to being political was when they were fatalistic and apocalyptic.

Dylan's new material caused Irwin Silber, editor of *Sing Out!* Magazine and a fiery veteran of the Old Left, to publish "An Open Letter to Bob Dylan" in which he noted with disfavor the singer's new songs which seemed "to be all inner-directed now, inner-probing, self-conscious – maybe even a little maudlin or a little cruel on occasion." For Silber and some other folk critics, introspection equaled acceptance of the political status quo. So far as they were concerned, one had no right to sing of self while others were being lynched. Silber went on to say that "some of the paraphenalia of fame" – code for *commercialism* – was getting in the way of Dylan continuing to do good work. Silence on political topics meant surrender and acquiescence.

Dylan thought otherwise. So too did Johnny Cash, who performed at Newport in '64 (with electric backup) and who penned an editorial in which he called Dylan a "poet troubador," urging critics to "shut up ... and let him sing." In an interview, Dylan told Nat Hentoff he thought he was pretty much done with "finger pointin' songs." In his book *Hard Rain*, critic Tim Riley notes of *Another Side of Bob Dylan* that: "As a set, the songs constitute a decisive act of noncommitment to issue-bound protest, to tradition-bound folk music and the possessive bonds of its audience." Luminscent poetry such as that offered by the cut "Chimes of Freedom" – itself a harbinger of so much which was to come from Dylan soon after – startled the ears of the core folk audience almost as much, if not more, than would the feedback of an electric guitar.

During his set at the '64 Festival, Johnny Cash performed Dylan's decidedly non-political "Don't Think Twice, It's All Right," and told the audience he and his band had "been doing it on our shows all over the country to tell the folks about Bob, that we think he's the best songwriter of the age since Pete Seeger."

Dylan himself had come to view his songs as something other than folk music simply-defined, and something other than mere protest music. He viewed his work, in fact, as something more important: songs *within the tradition,* albeit tradition far more broadly defined than Alan Lomax would have it.

In Dylan's view, traditional music had endured and grown through the years because it addressed universal themes of love and death and cosmic suffering (as opposed to limited political themes), and because it had been a present and central element to the environments in which people, common people at least, had actually found themselves. This had once been cotton fields and kitchens and castle courtyards, but not anymore. Now it was television and the radio. As Dylan told Hentoff:

> ... folk music is a word I can't use. ... I have to think of all this as traditional music. Traditional music ... comes about from legends, Bibles, plagues, ... and death. There's nobody that's going to kill traditional music. All these songs about roses growing out of people's brains and lovers who are really geese and swans that turn into angels – they're not going to die. ... Songs like "Which Side Are You On?" and "I Love You, Porgy" – they're not folk music songs; they're political songs. They're *already* dead. Obviously, death is not very universally accepted. I mean, you'd think

that the traditional music people could gather from their songs that mystery – just plain simple mystery – is a fact, a traditional fact. ... But anyway, traditional music is too unreal to die. It doesn't need to be protected. Nobody's going to hurt it. In that music is the only true, valid death you can feel today off a record player. But like anything else in great demand, people try to own it. It has to do with a purity thing. I think its meaninglessness is holy.

Dylan believed tradition (in any form of art) became such and remained such because it was innate to human nature; because it addressed a fundamental spiritual or psychological need, telling stories and addressing problems common across cultures and generations. Dylan likewise viewed packaging as irrelevant. Timeless tales were valid regardless of medium: whether sung in a ballad, narrated in a novel, or projected on a screen. New songs, pictures, films, or literature which related to fundamental truths of the human experience were just as much in the "tradition" as were their many times great-great-grandparents: songs sung by ancient fires, paintings made on cave walls, and tales told by the bards of old. Songs and tales and films about Robin Hood, Jesse James, Pretty Boy Floyd – they all shared the same DNA.

Technology changed. And means of distribution changed. But the true human experience did not. And *commercialization*? Just a side-effect. *Commercial* simply meant reaching out to an audience in the modern sense. Even the ancient, anonymous maker of *Beowolf* had, presumably, wanted people to hear his story. Modern commercial media walked in lockstep with tradition, whether Lomax liked it or not.

It should be noted here that unlike Lomax, Seeger did not have any particular problem with commercialism, *per se*. Lomax tended to view the new crop of city singer-songwriters – people like Dylan, Phil Ochs, and Tom Paxton – as mere interlopers: tourists and Tin Pan Alley production cogs. He likewise viewed popular performance groups such as Peter, Paul, and Mary with the same suspicion. But Seeger saw the popularization of folk music, however much pasteurized, as a continuing of the tradition into the modern age: a natural evolution rather than a distortion or aberration. (An important point here:

Seeger's own most "commercial" songs – particularly "Where Have All the Flowers Gone?" and "Turn! Turn! Turn!" – were not at all specifically political, but rather in essence spiritual – and therefore timeless.)

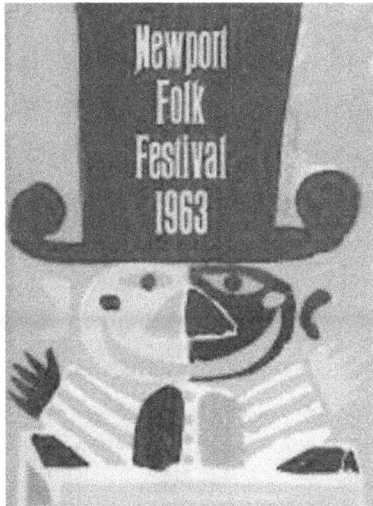

Bringing It All Back Home

Offer them what they secretly want, and they of course immediately become panic-stricken.
- Jack Kerouac

Recorded in January of 1965 and released in March, *Bringing It All Back Home* – Dylan's fifth album for Columbia – featured for the first time both acoustic and electric music, each on one side of the disk. On *Side One* Dylan combined raucous electric music with fantastic impressionist poetry to create such masterpieces as "Subterranean Homesick Blues." But he also included more tradition-bound lyrics to create the dogmatic "Maggie's Farm" – which, despite its fast moving electric groove, is by far the most traditionally-inspired cut on the entire album, far more so than any of the acoustic numbers on the flip side, these being "Mr. Tambourine Man," the highly symbolist "Gates of Eden," "It's All Over Now, Baby Blue," and "It's Alright Ma (I'm Only Bleeding)." Interestingly, many of the album's cuts, though electric, hardly qualify as "Rock." Nothing could be softer, for example, than the melodic "She Belongs to Me" or "Love Minus Zero/No Limit."

The album cover featured a spruced-up Dylan many had never seen before. A dapper Bob wears a black suit jacket and white shirt with blue pinstripes and cufflinks, and holds Albert Grossman's Persian cat. He sits in the formal living room of Grossman's Woodstock mansion. Grossman's seductive, cigarette-smoking, and very "Fifth Avenue" looking wife Sally gazes at him. On the table between them lay magazines and several record albums, the most prominent of which is one entitled *The Folk Blues of Eric Von Schmidt*.

Von Schmidt was a close friend of Dylan's and a superb acoustic blues stylist. He was also an out-standing graphic artist in the tradition of his father, Harold Von Schmidt, a prominent illustrator who – like his colleague Norman Rockwell – did much work for *The Saturday Evening Post*. Eric Von Schmidt had been raised in affluent Westport, Connecticut and as a young man studied art in Florence on a Fulbright Scholarship. Upon his return from Europe in 1957 he took up residence near Harvard University, painted, and became an integral part of the local Cambridge folk scene – which is where he met Dylan. Von Schmidt was to spend most of his life focusing on his painting, and through the years did cover art for albums by Joan Baez, Cisco Houston, and others. *The Folk Blues of Eric Von Schmidt* – featuring Richard Fariña and Dylan accompanying Von Schmidt – is one of only two albums he ever recorded.

Von Schmidt served as co-moderator with Lomax at the Newport workshop where Lomax and Grossman savaged each other. The workshop not only included Paul Butterfield and his group of Chicago bluesmen, but also Bill Monroe and his Bluegrass Boys, Sam and Kirk McGee, Son House, Memphis Slim, Willie Dixon, Spider John Koerner, Tony Glover (filling in for Josh White, who was ill), and Mance Lipscomb.

The Paul Butterfield Blues Band was headed by the classically trained flautist turned blues singer and harmonica player Paul Butterfield, who had been mentored in his latter passion by none other than Muddy Waters. Butterfield was joined by Mike Bloomfield, a superb blues guitarist who was the scion of a wealthy family from Chicago's North Side.

Bloomfield's mentors and supporters included not only Muddy Waters, but also Buddy Guy.

On the topic of how authentic it was for a white Jewish boy from a wealthy family to play the blues, Bloomfield commented: "It's natural. Black people suffer externally in this country. Jewish people suffer internally. The suffering's the mutual fulcrum of the blues."

Second guitarist Elvin Bishop, also outstanding, had been raised in Iowa and Oklahoma and attended the Univeristy of Chicago where he'd won a full scholarship based on his status as a National Merit Scholar, studying physics. Alabama's Sam Lay – a veteran of bands backing Howlin' Wolf, Little Walter, Willie Dixon, and Muddy Waters – covered the drums. Jerome Arnold – the only black man in the group – covered bass. Arnold was the brother of blues great Billy Boy Arnold and blues harmonica player Gus Arnold.

The Butterfield Band was scheduled to perform last at the Von Schmidt/Lomax *Blues Origins and Offshoots* workshop. Von Schmidt and Lomax took turns introducing each performer or group of performers, explaining exactly how the musical styles of each represented some element which fed into blues repertoire, topicality, or technique. All the performers before Butterfield and crew performed without amplification. When Butterfield and his cohorts began setting up their amplifiers and Sam Lay's drum kit, which took a while, Von Schmidt – preparing to introduce them – acquiesced to a request from Lomax that he, instead of Von Schmidt, say a few words.

Lomax's words turned out to be mocking words. In presenting the band, Lomax took it upon himself to deliver a five-minute mini-lecture concerning the origins of the blues, a talk during which he defined the music as a natural, organic force arising not from imitation, but from genuine experience and culture. Lomax closed by inviting workshop participants not to enjoy the band, but rather to sit in judgment as to whether the imitative product of Butterfield and friends – inspired not by life but by recordings of "the real thing" – qualified as blues at all.

As Lomax walked off the stage, and before the band began to play, an affronted Grossman (who would soon take on the band as clients) rose from the audience and challenged him. Lomax shoved Grossman out of his way. Grossman shoved back. And on it went until broken up by Lay and others. (The next day, Lomax would convene a meeting of the folk Festival's board – which no longer included Grossman – for the purpose of voting to ban Grossman from the Festival grounds, only to have this move vetoed by primary Festival organizers George Wein and Pete Seeger. Both Wein and Seeger, by the way, had [at Peter Yarrow's urging] approved the appearance of Butterfield's quintet, otherwise they would not have been invited to participate in the Festival in the first place.)

Following the fight, the Butterfield Band's subsequent set – supported by amplifiers set up on the informal plywood platform of the workshop – was warmly received by the Festival crowd. Butterfield's wailing harmonica and Bloomfield's and Bishop's virtuoso blues guitar riffs were greeted with enthusiastic applause. One day later, being interviewed by filmmaker Murray Lerner, Bloomfield – probably harkening back to Lomax's comments – noted that though he admittedly had never suffered the hard life of a black man, he could nevertheless play the blues, which was universal. The *world*, after all, was hard.

In a demonstration of just how quickly a myth or urban legend can be invented and distributed (itself a strident example of the pure "folk process"), word soon spread that Lomax, in knocking the Butterfield Band, had meant by this to condemn the use of electric instruments. Nothing could have been further from the truth.

Despite the fact of Lomax's obnoxious and auto-cratic snobbishness, the fact is he'd time and time again leveled the same criticism at *all* "copycats" and "popularisers" whom he saw as exploiting rather than expanding the folk tradition. Amplification had nothing to do with it.

In other years, Howlin' Wolf – an artist whom Lomax considered to be "genuine," born and raised "within the tradition" – played at the Festival with electric guitars, bass and drums, with Lomax among the first to praise his set, as did Seeger. In 1965, not only the Butterfield band but also the Chambers Brothers played thoroughly electric sets.

News of Grossman's and Lomax's tussle spread like wildfire, as did the supposition that it had been over electric vs. acoustic instruments. In this version, Lomax represented not an inflexible musicological purist but rather the "old guard" of the folk movement as exemplified by acoustic instruments, while Grossman represented the "new guard" as exemplified by electric amplification.

Neither banner was accurate. Neither group – "old guard" or "new guard" – had ever even been previously defined or articulated before this weekend. As has been noted earlier, the major rift between Grossman and Lomax was about commercialism, which Lomax saw as beeing toxic to authenticity. Ironically, the raw, straight-up, and ultimately authentic blues sound of the Butterfield band was hardly commercial at all.

A few of the Newport albums issued by Vanguard Records through the years.

All I Really Want To Do

All I can do is be me, whoever that is.
- Bob Dylan

Dylan – whose electric "Like a Rolling Stone" had been released only a few days earlier and whose latest album had, as noted, featured an entire side of electric cuts – arrived at Newport on the evening of the 23rd intending to play only acoustic music over the next two days and nights. He brought with him neither a band nor an electric guitar.

During the afternoon of the 24th, Dylan participated in the *Ballad Tree* workshop where he performed a profoundly non-electric version of "All I Really Want To Do" along with several other acoustic numbers. Only later, after he in his turn was told the evolving myth of the acoustic vs. electric altercation, did he decide to make his evening, July 25th performance into a statement against the newly defined "old guard." Woody, he told Grossman, wouldn't have shut any artist down, and Bob would be damn-ed if he'd let Lomax do so.

Thus everyone stepped through the looking-glass. Lines were drawn between two camps which were not, in fact, opposed. Amplified vs. acoustic music was a war that did not exist, even though an historic skirmish was about to be joined.

Preparations were hasty. Dylan convened a band consisting of Bloomfield, Butterfield, pianist Barry Goldberg, Butterfield drummer Sam Lay, bassist Jerome Arnold, and organist Al Kooper (the latter just happening to be attending the Festival). Kooper had played organ on the studio version of "Like a Rolling Stone" – along with Bloomfield on guitar – and was happy to repeat his performance on short notice. There was little time for rehearsal, and even less for the sound-check on the afternoon of the 25th.

Peter Yarrow ran the board at the sound-check, but was given little chance to get the levels right. Dylan played only a few bars of each of the songs he intended to perform. Dylan's rather chaotic, newly-gathered ensemble chimed along as best they could in a highly-improvisational manner. (Given its random and spontaneous nature, Dylan's electric set was to be

far more "traditional" than the sets of the many care-
fully-rehearsed "city" performers, all acoustic, who
were so warmly received throughout the weekend.)

Seeger, aware of and unbothered by "Bobby's"
decision to appear with Bloomfield and company,
heard the sound-check going on in the distance as he
worked with his elderly musicologist father Charles
Seeger and others at a folklore workshop, and was
glad to assume attention was being paid to details.
"Doing sound for amplified instruments is a lot more
tricky than doing it for acoustic music" he said years
later, "especially in an open air performance space."

The evening's performance opened with the Butterfield Blues Band *sans* Dylan – this appearance being a consolation prize after the band's originally-
scheduled performance at that afternoon's "New
Folks" concert got rained out. Other acts on the
evening's bill included the Beers Family, Len
Chandler, Cousin Emmy, Ronnie Gilbert (of the
Weavers), Fannie Lou Hamer, Jean Ritchie, Eric Von
Schmidt, and Peter, Paul, and Mary. In other words,
several of the performers were such as Lomax would
consider "genuine" traditionalists, with Len Chandler, Ronnie Gilbert, Von Schmidt, the Butterfield en-

semble, Dylan, and Peter, Paul, and Mary being the exceptions.

Butterfield and his comrades performed a strong set to a crowd that, while still filing into the Festival Field, was nevertheless appreciative. The band used its own amps only, performing without use of the house sound system. The omnidirectional microphones of brothers Maynard and Seymour Solomon, proprietors of Vanguard Records who had rights to record the Festival music – were also turned off, as the Solomon brothers were for the most part interested in recording "name" acts rather than strict traditionalists or newbies. Issuing from their own customized amp system, the Paul Butterfield Band's music was clear, discernable, smooth and crisp – and their reception gracious, despite electrification.

Throughout the day, the ever-evolving tale of the Grossman/Lomax fisticuffs had circulated widely. So had word that Dylan intended to draw a line in the sand, confronting Lomax and other "traditionalists" with the sound of a new generation: genuine revolution. As the evening built, so did the anticipation.

Applause greeted Dylan and his protégés as, near the close of the evening, they entered the stage and plugged-in. After a moment of tuning, and without a word from Bob, the group dove into a horribly mixed and somewhat discordant, random version of "Maggie's Farm."

Perhaps mercifully, the extremely mediocre, under-rehearsed performance could hardly be discerned amidst feedback generated between the conflicting stage amplifiers and house sound system. The mix on both was bad, as was the initial idea of combining the two systems in the first place. The result resembled static white noise amidst which both the song's tune and most of Bob's singing were nearly totally drowned out, as were the boos and shouts of "Turn it down!" coming from the crowd. "We can't hear you!" shouted Von Schmidt. Another close Dylan friend, Mark Spoelstra, would recall: "All you could hear was Al Kooper and the guitar and the bass and this kind of agonizing sort of a scream of a voice, but you had *no idea* what he was saying."

Yarrow almost immediately clambered onto the stage and frantically sought to adjust the balances on the amplifiers. He also endeavored to move the several microphones which disiasterously stood too close to the pickups of Bloomfield's Futura and Dylan's Thunderbird electric guitars.

In fact, the need was not to turn anything down, but rather to simply turn the competing house sound system *off*, as had been done for the earlier Butterfield set. The feedback would have disappeared instantly. But this was not going to happen. Maynard and Seymour Solomon's microphones were synced with the house sound system. While they'd been completely willing to skip recording the relatively unknown Butterfield group, they were simply not going to go without the Festival star, Dylan. Killing the house system was not an option.

Realizing the disquiet of the audience, Dylan hardly paused at all between songs, quickly moving into an equally indiscernible performance of "Like a Rolling Stone," this followed by something he was then calling "Phantom Engineer," a song which later became "It Takes A Lot to Laugh, It Takes a Train to Cry."

Backstage, just a few moments into the experiment in feedback which was supposed to be "Maggie's Farm," Seeger's father Charles winced with pain as the feedback pounded into his twin hearing aids.

Seeger, meanwhile, moved quickly to the soundboard with a request to lower the volume on the house system, this to hopefully alleviate at least some of the feedback. "No. This is the way they want it," came the reply from engineers Paul Rothschild and Joe Boyd.

"I don't know who *they* was," Seeger recalled. (In fact, *they* were the Solomon brothers.) "I was furious that the sound was so distorted you could not understand a word Bobby was singing. He was singing a great song, 'Maggie's Farm.' *A great song.* But you couldn't understand it. ... I was so mad I said 'If I had an axe I'd cut the cable right now.' I really was that mad. But I wasn't against Bob going electric." (Three months after the Festival, the Byrds would score a number one hit with their all electric version of Seeger's "Turn! Turn! Turn!" – a version Seeger was quick to praise. The record was a follow-up to the band's previous hit, their electric version of Dylan's "Mr. Tambourine Man.")

The apocryphal story of the evening says that Seeger actually did try to cut the power with an axe. As absolutely every actual witness to the backstage drama attests, this simply did not happen.

The most truly bitter response came not from backstage, but from the audience itself. Different witnesses offer different opinions on the source of the crowd's loud animosity – a shrill round of hisses and boos which continued as Dylan stalked off after his third number, visibly shaken and upset. Some, like Oscar Brand, believed it to be a reaction to the electric performance and the commercialism it seemed, to some, to represent. "It was the antithesis of what the Festival was supposed to be doing," he recalled. "The electric guitar represented capitalism ... the people who were selling out." Other observers suggest – probably closer to the mark – that the majority of people were simply annoyed about the terrible sound, or about the brevity of Dylan's performance, or perhaps more likely a combination of both these factors. Dylan's set was supposed to last 45 minutes. It ended after less than 15.

As for commercialism being the thrust behind any move from acoustic instruments to electrified instruments, consider the facts. Like Seeger's Weavers in the 1950s, acoustic performers such as Dylan and Baez and Peter, Paul, and Mary were selling records by the hundreds of thousands – records issued on

major labels, records scoring as hits – and com-
manding high concert fees. At the same time, electric
Chicago blues such as that purveyed by Bloomfield,
Butterfield and others was about as likely to hit the
pop charts as a blind batter was to hit a home-run.
Still, oversimplification or not, Brand's analysis cer-
tainly reflected the attitude of at least some of the
Newport audience. Along with shouts of "Turn it
down!" there had also been taunts: "Judas!" and "Go
back to *American Bandstand!*"

Regardless of the range of audience reactions and
complaints, all were at least somewhat sated once
Yarrow managed to lure Dylan out to do a few
acoustic tunes.

Another urban legend that has sprung up about
this night is that Dylan appeared back on stage carrying an acoustic guitar borrowed from Johnny Cash.
This would been somewhat hard to pull off since
Cash – who'd appeared at the '64 Festival – was a
thousand miles away from Newport on July 25th,
1965.

The guitar Dylan carried was his own. And the
applause which greeted him was deafening. Along
with his guitar, he wore his standard harmonica hold-

er around his neck, but soon realized the harmonica it held, which he'd used for his electric set, was the wrong key for the acoustic songs he now intended to sing. "Has anybody got an E harmonica?" he shouted into the crowd. *"Anybody.* An E harmonica. Just throw them all up." Half a dozen came pelting over him. "Thank you!" he shouted, bending down and reaching for the nearest one.

Dylan performed only two songs before exiting the Newport stage for what would turn out to be a 37 year hiatus. First, "Mr. Tamborine Man." Then, perhaps tellingly, "It's All Over Now, Baby Blue." Later on, at an after-party for the musicians, Seeger and Dylan talked quietly in a corner. Seeger commiserated with the upset and distracted Dylan who seemed unable to process or understand the evening's unfortunate sequence of events. Whatever statement he'd been trying to make had been quite literally distorted – in part by idle, uninformed chatter, and in part by pure electrical current in the form of fuzz and feedback. Instead of the medium being the message, the medium had contorted, dismantled and defeated the message.

Further into the evening, as the Chambers Brothers stepped up to play some dance music, Maria
Muldaur strolled over to where Bob sulked in a corner and asked him to dance with her. "I'd dance with
you, Maria," he answered, "but my hands are on
fire."

Not long afterward, *Sing Out!* Magazine's Silber
condemned Dylan as having become a "pawn in his
own game. He has given up his companions for the
companionship of the charts." But music critic Paul
Nelson, writing in the same publication, insisted
those who rejected Dylan's latest work "were choos-
ing suffocation over invention and adventure, back-
wards over forwards, a dead hand instead of a live
one."

The Newport *folk festival* Songbook

edited by JEAN RITCHIE with a foreword by PETE SEEGER

Here are the songs and singers
of the Newport Folk Festival!
57 different songs by 57 different
artists, with the story behind
each song, the facts behind each
artist. Photos, illustrations, write-up
of Theodore Bikel, Johnny Cash,
Judy Collins, Pete Seeger
and many others.

114 PAGES OF FOLK SONGS! *Alfred Music* CO. INC., N.Y. PRICE $2.95 IN U.S.A.

Much Ado About Nothing Much

Tradition is a guide and not a jailer.
- W. Somerset Maugham

Seeger's 1967 album for Columbia, *Wasit Deep in the Big Muddy and Other Love Songs*, included the Blues Project's Danny Kalb playing backup electric guitar. Dylan's 1968 album for Columbia, *John Wesley Harding*, signaled Dylan's return to acoustic music. In 2006, the rocker Bruce Springstein recorded an entire album of Seeger covers: *The Seeger Sessions*. In 1974, sitting at lunch in a Malibu restaurant with Seeger, Arlo Guthrie, and Guthrie's and Seeger's manager Harold Leventhal, Dylan reminisced about the historic night at Newport in 1965 and summed it up as "bullshit, total bullshit. Nobody got what was going on. Not even me."

In the years 1992 and '93 Dylan released two albums featuring solo performances of strictly roots material. These were "Good as I Been To You" and "World Gone Wrong." Dylan covered songs from

Blind Willie McTell, Charley Patton, Lonnie Johnson, Blind Blake, the Mississippi Shieks, and others. He was, he said, regaining his artistic balance by drinking afresh from the well out of which he'd sprung. A writer for the *New York Times* commented that listening to these two albums was "a little like watching someone rewire an old house." Not that traditional music had ever left Dylan's repertoire. Indeed, by his reckoning it was all he ever had done, or ever would do.

Writing of *Good As I Been To You* in *Rolling Stone*, David Wild commented:

> If your memory serves you well, you will recall that Bob Dylan was unplugged decades before MTV made it hip to be musically square again. Later, of course, he would inspire generations of singer-songwriters to plug in. So when in 1992 Dylan decides to cut a totally acoustic record of traditional folk and blues material that features only his own voice, guitar and harmonica, he is just about the last artist who could be accused of jumping on the musical bandwagon. After all, he helped build

the wagon.

In its stripped-down intensity, *Good As I Been to You* recalls the midshow acoustic segments that in recent years have been a consistent highlight of Dylan's Neverending Tour. Even more than that, the album's intimate, almost offhand approach suggests what it would be like to sit backstage with his Bobness while he runs through a set of some of his favorite old songs. This is a passionate, at times almost ragged piece of work that seems to have been recorded rather than produced in any conventional sense.

Only a quarter of a century late, this is the sort of album the people who booed Dylan's decision to go electric wanted from him.

Dylan made a much-hyped return to the Newport Folk Festival in 2002 – ironically just a couple of weeks after the death of Alan Lomax. "With his highly anticipated return to the Newport Folk Festival," wrote critic David Read, "Bob Dylan presented his audience not with a musical masterpiece nor any acknowledgment that this was a special gig, but rather the silly sight of himself wearing a wig. ... Was this ... just a goof to see how much palaver the wig (and fake beard) will generate in the media and elsewhere, his Newport '65 performance having established the gold standard for much ado about nothing much?"

Dylan and his band plowed through a two-hour set, including: "Subterranean Homesick Blues," "Desolation Row," "Positively 4th Street," "The Wicked Messenger," "Like a Rolling Stone," and "Mr. Tambourine Man." The performers had just come off a 12-week touring hiatus. They sounded quite under-rehearsed – far from seamless. Dylan said not a word between songs, and acted for all the world as if this, to him, was just another show. And it probably was. Although he played several numbers with simple acoustic guitar accompaniment, this was a standard part of his set list at the time and not a special concession to Newport. The wig under his white cowboy hat went unexplained, as did the fake beard.

For 14 years, from 1971 to 1985, there'd been no Newport Folk Festival. By 2002, the Festival – now corporate sponsored – had come very far from its roots. 90% of the performers were singer-songwriters. And they were often "folk" only in the loosest sense that they either played acoustic music or at least did not rock too fiercely, such as when the Allman Brothers and the Pixies brought toned down versions of their music to the Newport stage. "Name" artists ruled the day, and commanded hefty performance fees. The gig was professional for all who appeared, not the least for Dylan. And the audience was there to be entertained, not proselytized for worthy causes or instructed on the art of the Highland Flute. In a sense, the Festival had become what Dylan would have liked it to have been in '65: a venue without pretenses, messages, or cons of any kind. (Although Dylan was, for the record, the only artist at the Festival to have his own merchandise tent.)

The most important part of Dylan's appearance was probably the meditations it inspired in the press and elsewhere: the key message being that the more things (including Dylan) change, the more they stay the same. Call it *tradition*. "Rather than the dissonant break with the past that nearly everyone took his performance to be at the time," wrote the *New York Times's* Tom Piazza, "Newport 1965 was emblematic of Dylan's continuity as an artist. Nothing that is a part of him would be disowned; rather than breaking with his influences, he would make room for all of them."

No truer words.

EJR
Wickford, Rhode Island
2 June 2015

Acknowledgments

Mucho thanks: Robin Appel, Eric Liberman, Stephen Sweeney, Rosanne Giardina Simpson, Kevin Renehan, Pauline Kentridge, Chad M. Horn, Nora Krapf, Katherine Schowalter, Sharon Gamba, Mark and Katrina Cottom, Chris Davis, Alice Lima, Dennis Doherty, Jeanne Eliades, Don "Winker" Emmons, Debbie Russo, Peter Ginna, Arthur Goldwag, Kevin King, Kevin Crotty, Adrienne Friedland, Howard Marcus, Eina Fishman, Bob Killian, Dino Bonacasa, Joanne Zurlo, Robert Crooke, Paul Christensen, Kathie Wycoff, Kitty Hendrix, Diane Court, Susan Bricker, Herb McCormick, Scott Wachter, Susan de la Torre, Mike Stanko and Karen Zang, Nick Hahn, Elizabeth Woodman, Eileen Charbonneau, Jimmy Ferraro, Diane Pineiro-Zucker, Rita Hurault, David Gans, William Ramage, Eleanor Walden, Peter Caldwell, Allen Josephs, Bruce Holley, Ency Austin, and Bill and Roberta Schnoor. And God bless the beautiful Jean Ritchie who passed on the first of June at age 92, just as I was finishing this book.

About The Author

Edward Renehan serves as Managing Director of the publishing firm New Street Communications, which includes the subsidiaries Dark Hall Press and New Street Nautical Audio. He is the author of many books including *The Secret Six* (Crown, 1995), *The Lion's Pride* (Oxford University Press, 1998), *The Kennedys at War* (Doubleday, 2002), *Dark Genius of Wall Street* (Basic Books, 2005), and *Pete Seeger vs. The Un-Americans: A Tale of the Blacklist* (New Street, 2014). His articles and reviews have appeared in such publications as the *San Francisco Chronicle*, Hearst's *Veranda* and the *Wall Street Journal*. He lives near Newport, RI.

ALSO OF INTEREST
FROM NEW STREET

Pete Seeger vs. The Un-Americans: A Tale of the Blacklist
By Edward Renehan
"A truly enjoyable and informative read." - Steve Buscemi,
actor/director

Capsized: Jim Nalepka's Epic 119 Day Survival Voyage
Aboard the Rose Noëlle
By Steven Callahan
"Soulful, emotional … earnest and engrossing." - KIRKUS

Beast: A Slightly Irreverent Tale About Cancer (And Other
Assorted Anecdotes)
By James Capuano
"A surprisingly life-affirming tale." - Susan Sarandon, actress

Hemingway's Paris: Our Paris?
by H.R. Stoneback
"Stoneback's lyrical prose takes the reader inside the soul of
Hemingway's Paris, penetrating the surface of guide-books to
reveal tantalizing secrets." - A.E. Hotchner